Sixty Reasons Why You Should Hire the Sexagenarian

W. Scott Moore

Eleos Press

Rogersville, Alabama

First Printing

Sixty Reasons Why You Should Hire the Sexagenarian

Author: W. Scott Moore, B.B.A., M. Div., D. Min.
© 2014 by Eleos Press www.eleospress.com

Cover Art: W. Scott Moore
Cover Design: W. Scott Moore
Interior Formatting: Eleos Press
www.eleospress.com
Also available in eBook form

Most of the descriptors used in this book are the author's. Additional descriptors have been taken from "Positive Personality Adjectives List: List of 100 common personality adjectives that describe people positively,"
https://www.englishclub.com/vocabulary/adjectives-personality-positive.htm, site visited on 9/20/2014.

ISBN-13: 978-0692299517

PRINTED IN THE UNITED STATES OF AMERICA

Introduction

Did the title of this book catch your attention? It really is quite innocent. You see, a *sexagenarian* is simply "a person whose age is in the sixties."[1] In other words, someone who is between 60 and 69 years of age.

Being a sexagenarian myself, I thought that this book might pique the interest of two main audiences:

1. Others, like myself, that are interested in remaining in, or reentering, the workforce in order to make a positive difference in our world.

2. Employers that may have previously missed a "goldmine" of potential in overlooking a member of this prestigious group in the hiring process.

---

[1] MERRIAM-WEBSTER'S COLLEGIATE DICTIONARY AND THESAURUS, DELUXE AUDIO EDITION®, Version 2.5, Copyright © Merriam-Webster, Incorporated, 47 Federal Street, P.O. Box 28l, Springfield, MA 01102.

Additionally, federal law has clearly spoken regarding this matter[2]:

It shall be unlawful for an employer:

(1) to fail or refuse to hire or to discharge any individual or otherwise discriminate against any individual with respect to his compensation, terms, conditions, or privileges of employment, because of such individual's age;

(2) to limit, segregate, or classify his employees in any way which would deprive or tend to deprive any individual of employment opportunities or otherwise adversely affect his status as an employee, because of such individual's age; or

(3) to reduce the wage rate of any employee in order to comply with this chapter.

You might ask, "Why 'pull out the big guns'? Why drag the government into this otherwise friendly

---

[2] "The Age Discrimination Act of 1967," http://www.eeoc.gov/laws/statutes/adea.cfm, site visited on 9/22/2014.

discussion?" Because, quite simply, *before* the law was written and implemented, some employers had a rather biased view toward employing older workers—those over the age of 40—that were, quite honestly, in other respects qualified to do the job for which they were hiring.

Admittedly, not every sexagenarian will possess all sixty of the character traits outlined in this book. Some will possess all sixty and more. Enjoy this book. Let it open the door for a profitable relationship between employers and their regimen of seasoned employees.

1

Adaptable

Willing to try new things and new ways of doing things

W. Scott Moore

2

Alert

Scientists tell us that, as we age,
we require less sleep

3

Apolitical

Disinterested in office politics

W. Scott Moore

4

Bargains

Typically have an additional source of income

5

Broad-minded

Not confined to "the norm"

W. Scott Moore

Calm

Personally relaxed and have a calming influence on those around them

7

Careful

Pay attention to details

W. Scott Moore

8

Communicative

Have mastered the techniques of listening to others and of sharing their own ideas

9

Compassionate

Understand your concerns and the concerns of others on your team

W. Scott Moore

10

Confident

Know *who* they are and *why* they
are there

11

Conservative

Believe in the free market and in
helping their employers to succeed

12

Decisive

Capable of making decisions based
upon experience

13

Eager

Many of them are looking for work
and are available to start today

W. Scott Moore

14

Easygoing

Less likely to become involved in personal and work-place drama

15

Energized

Concerned about your company's reputation and its future

W. Scott Moore

16

Experienced

Wisdom is associated with age

17

Flexible

Willing to work part-time; you can
plug them in wherever needed

18

Frugal

Know the relative values of
products and/or services

19

Generous

Willing to invest their time and
their money in what they believe

W. Scott Moore

20

Genuine

More concerned with character
than dress and appearance

21

Givers

Not takers from your company/organization

W. Scott Moore

22

Harmonious

Make the effort to get along well
with others

23

Helpful

Desire to meet the needs of others

24

Honest

Live by a moral compass

25

Independent

Able to work without close supervision

W. Scott Moore

26

Intelligent

Know the basics of reading, writing, and arithmetic

27

Intuitive

Instinctively know what you want
from them and how to provide it

28

Locals

Their family members live nearby;
less likely to move away.

29

Loyal

Thankful, rather than believing that you are lucky to have them

W. Scott Moore

30

Manageable

Less likely to "buck the system"

31

Mediators

Willing to work with people to help find common ground

W. Scott Moore

32

Mentors

Willing to help you lead the other
younger, less-experienced, workers

33

Modest

Willing to share the praise for a job well done

W. Scott Moore

34

Motivated

Truly enjoy their work

35

Organized

Prioritize; they know what is
important, and what is not

36

Passionate

Believe in your company and its products and/or services

37

Patient

Have learned to endure under less-than-ideal circumstances

W. Scott Moore

38

Persistent

Have learned how to deal with rejection

39

Polite

Grew up in a day in which their
parents instilled good manners

W. Scott Moore

40

Practical

Know what works—and what doesn't

41

Pro-active

Believe the adage, "A stitch in time saves nine"

W. Scott Moore

42

Punctual

Have learned to be on time for
their responsibilities

43

Realistic

Recognize, and adjust to, their limitations

W. Scott Moore

44

Reliable

You can depend upon them

45

Resourceful

Bring years of experience to the table

46

Sacrificial

Willing to do more and work longer
hours than is expected of them

47

Scarce

Rare; they are, therefore, more
valuable as members of your team

W. Scott Moore

48

Self-starters

Grew up when work was not
considered to be a 4-letter word

49

Short-termers

Perform well, without becoming
homesteaders in your company

W. Scott Moore

50

Sincere

What you see is what you get

51

Sociable

Friendly, good-natured,
personable, amicable

W. Scott Moore

52

Stable

Have moved beyond the need for
job-hopping

53

Steady

Know how to pace themselves

54

Subservient

Are willing to do the most menial of tasks

55

Survivors

Have learned to "hang on" during difficult circumstances

W. Scott Moore

56

Symbiotic

Their work for you will be mutually
beneficial

57

Trustworthy

Their "name" is extremely
important to them

W. Scott Moore

58

Temperate

Unlikely to miss work because of
various chemical dependencies

59

Unassuming

Are not seeking to displace you on
their climb up the corporate ladder

W. Scott Moore

60

Versatile

Capable of multi-tasking

A Note to Fellow

Sexagenarians

I hope you have found this book to be helpful. I also hope that it will become a useful tool for you as you seek to continue in, or return to, the workforce.

I would like to give you a free tool—a key— for effectively using this book to your advantage. I learned this key many years ago in sales training. It is called a *unit of conviction*. A *unit of conviction*, simply put, is a four-stage process of convincing someone to make the right decision: feature, benefit, evidence, pin down.

- Feature—something that describes the product—in this case, you—that you are trying to sell.

- Benefit—an explanation as to how this "feature" will be advantageous to the potential "buyer"— your prospective employer.

- Evidence—the proof you offer for the benefit(s) you are claiming. There are seven kinds of evidence used in selling:

  1. Facts and statistics (self-explanatory)
  2. Exhibit—for instance, the volcano project that often appears in science fairs
  3. Visualization—a word picture
  4. Personal experience (self-explanatory)
  5. Demonstration—showing how it works
  6. Analogy—using "like" or "as" to compare your product (yourself) to someone or something else
  7. Testimonial—what someone else has said about your product (you) that establishes the benefit you are claiming

- Pin down—a simple statement, such as, "That's important, isn't it," or, "You can see why this is important."

Let me walk you through this one. The first reason that employers should hire a sexagenarian is that:

1. **FEATURE**: "I am *adaptable*—willing to try new things and new ways of doing things."

2. **BENEFIT**: "If you choose to hire me, your methods will become my methods."

3. **EVIDENCE** (in this example, #4—personal experience): "When I was in my twenties, I thought that I knew everything. I have since discovered that I have a lot to learn, and I am thoroughly enjoying the journey!"

4. **PIN DOWN**: While nodding, "I'm sure you would agree that being adaptable is important to any business or organization."

You *could* do this exercise for all sixty of the following traits but that, I'm afraid, would become a rather unenjoyable task. I recommend that you pick out the three or four traits that most clearly describe you personally. Next, write out the unit of conviction for each one, using all seven types of evidence. Finally, select the type of evidence that most clearly and powerfully establishes your assertion.

Once you have formulated your units of conviction, use them lavishly. Practice using them with friendly audiences (family members and colleagues), place them prominently in the cover letters you send with your résumés, and sprinkle them conspicuously throughout job interviews.

You might consider buying several copies of this book (hint, hint) to give to your friends to help *them* in *their* ongoing searches for employment. And you might even buy some to slip in with your résumés as an added bonus to your prospective employer.

Have fun, and happy job hunting!

W. Scott Moore

Bibliography

MERRIAM-WEBSTER'S COLLEGIATE
    DICTIONARY AND THESAURUS,
    DELUXE AUDIO EDITION®, Version
    2.5, Copyright © Merriam-
    Webster, Incorporated, 47 Federal Street,
    P.O. Box 28l, Springfield, MA 01102.

"Positive Personality Adjectives List: List of 100
    common personality adjectives that describe
    people positively,"
    https://www.englishclub.com/vocabulary/adj
    ectives-personality-positive.htm, site visited
    on 9/20/2014.

"The Age Discrimination Act of 1967,"
    http://www.eeoc.gov/laws/statutes/adea.
    cfm, site visited on 9/22/2014.

For More Information:

For more information about this book, or to publish your own book with Eleos Press, contact the author.

W. Scott Moore, B.B.A., M.Div., D.Min., has published nine of his own books. He has also published, edited, and revised numerous books for many other authors. In addition to his writing and publishing, he is currently serving as the senior pastor of a rural church in north Alabama.

Personal email address: moorescott@aol.com

Website: www.eleospress.com

Amazon Author Central page:
http://www.amazon.com/W.-Scott-Moore/e/B006FHNVPS/ref=sr_ntt_srch_lnk_1?qid=1411395795&sr=8-1